George Best

U N S E E N   A R C H I V E S

George Best

UNSEEN ARCHIVES

Tim Hill

Photographs by the

p

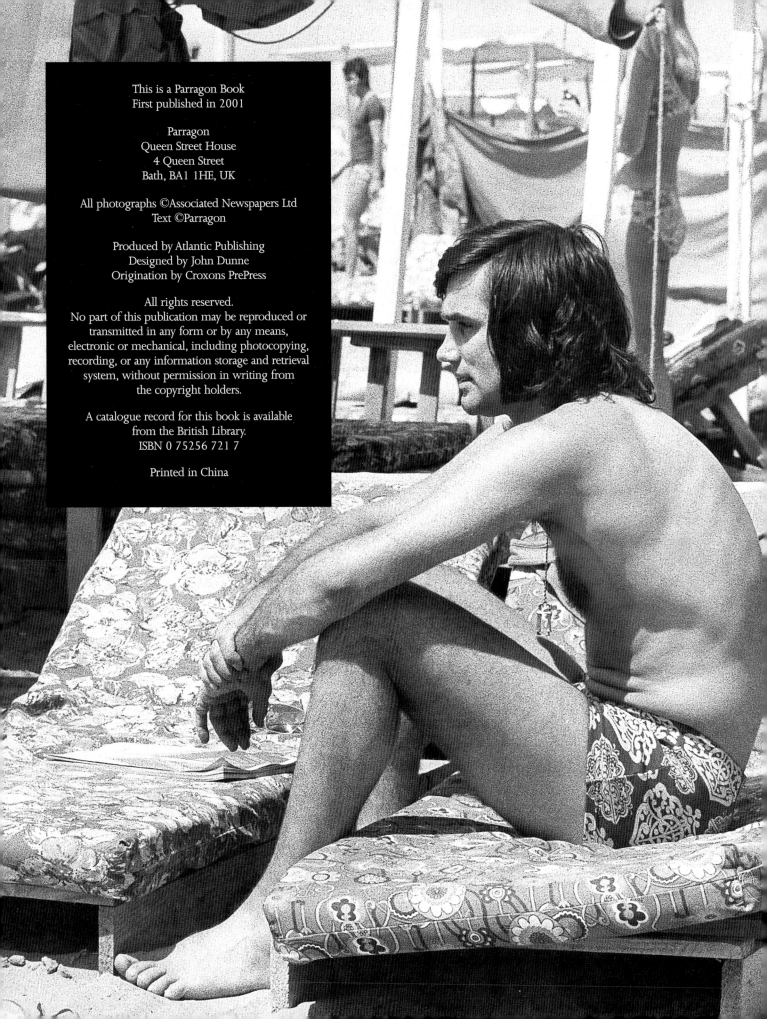

This is a Parragon Book
First published in 2001

Parragon
Queen Street House
4 Queen Street
Bath, BA1 1HE, UK

Produced by Atlantic Publishing
Designed by John Dunne
Origination by Croxons PrePress

A catalogue record for this book is available
from the British Library.
ISBN 0 75256 721 7

Printed in China

Contents

Acknowledgements

The photographs from this book are from the archives of the *Daily Mail*.
The pleasure this book will give is a tribute to the dedication of the staff, past and present,
in the Picture Library at Associated Newspapers.

Particular thanks to
Steve Torrington, Dave Sheppard, Brian Jackson, Alan Pinnock, Paul Rossiter
and all the staff.

Thanks also to
Christine Hoy, John Dunne, Cliff Salter, Richard Betts, Peter Wright,
Trevor Bunting and Simon Taylor.

Belfast Boy

'I have found a genius'

Manchester United scout Bob Bishop was unequivocal in the telegram he sent to Old Trafford after watching 15-year-old George Best in action. Matt Busby had already been United boss for fifteen years and was well used to having a stream of excellent young players recommended to him. Indeed, a decade earlier he adopted a policy of scouring the country for the cream of schoolboy talent. Busby had moulded a wonderful team which won the FA Youth Cup five times in a row, not to mention back-to-back League titles. In short, the man who had assembled the brilliant 'Babes' side wasn't about to be taken in by hyperbole and the casual use of superlatives.

Yet when Busby finally got to see George Best play, he fully endorsed the epithet Bob Bishop had chosen to use. Busby had had Bobby Charlton and Duncan Edwards at Old Trafford; he knew what Finney and Puskas could do; he had seen the great Real Madrid side that included di Stefano and Gento; yet he was to hail George as the most naturally gifted player ever to grace the football field.

Honing his skills

If not quite born with a ball at his feet, Best certainly started honing his magical skills as soon as he could walk unaided. Growing up on Belfast's Cregagh Estate there were the usual school matches and street games, in which he excelled. More interesting, perhaps, is the way in which he revelled in solitary practice. Hour after hour, often late into the night, he would be found hitting a ball against walls and garage doors. He would set himself difficult targets, not resting until he had achieved them. If there was a skill or trick that he couldn't master straight away, he would practise assiduously until he had mastered it.

A good example of Best's dedicated approach to skills training was the way he taught himself to hit a tennis ball against gutters and doorknobs and make it rebound straight to him. It was a skill that he adapted to great effect in the professional game. The non-uniform surface was now defenders' shins, and he regularly played neat, deliberate one-twos off them. Best may have been blessed with sublime natural ability, but he also had an indefatigable appetite for practice.

The combination of immense skill and single-minded dedication was bound to attract interest from scouts. Several looked at him but Best cut a frail figure on the pitch. Even when he reached his teens he remained stick-thin, weighing in at just six stones. It counted against him.

The timing wasn't propitious for a player of Best's stature either. In the early 1960s many coaches were focusing on the 'power game' - hard running, tough tackling, physically intimidating. Matt Busby was one of the few who saw such a move as a retrograde step. He understood all too well the importance of strength, pace and power, but these were subordinate to the primary attribute: skill.

Cregagh Boys Club

One of the chief exponents of the power game was Don Revie's Leeds United side, and perhaps it is no coincidence that Leeds was one of the clubs who took one look at this young waif from Belfast and felt that he wouldn't be able to withstand the rigours of the modern game.

Bob Bishop also had his doubts. He purposely arranged a game between Best's Cregagh Boys Club and his own team, Boyland, which was one of Northern Ireland's top youth sides. Many of the Boyland players were 18, yet 15-year-old Best was the star of the show, scoring twice in a 4-2 win. The last shred of doubt was removed from Bishop's mind and the telegram was duly dispatched to Old Trafford.

Having all but given up hope of making it as a professional, and with an apprenticeship in the printing trade waiting, Best suddenly found himself invited for a 2-week trial with the most glamorous club in British football in the summer of 1961. It was bound to be an intimidating prospect for a 15-year-old, although at least he didn't have goggle-eyed hero-worship to contend with. Like many of his contemporaries, Best followed an English League club as well as a local side. His allegiance at home was to Glentoran; on the mainland it was Molyneux, not Old Trafford, where the young George's affections lay.

United's young hopefuls

He travelled to Manchester by boat with another young hopeful, Eric McMordie. It should have been the realization of a dream, yet the sojourn lasted barely twenty-four hours. No one was sent to meet them, so they climbed into a taxi and asked to be taken to Old Trafford. 'Which one?' came the reply. Discovering that Old Trafford was also an illustrious cricketing venue ought to have been a trivial, even comical incident. But for two young boys far from home for the first time in their lives it was disconcerting. Nor did things improve when they eventually made it to the ground. The boys felt overawed, out of their depth and homesick. They shared their misgivings in their digs that evening, and decided to head back to Belfast the following day.

George's second chance

Best's parents, Dick and Ann, were neither pushy nor interested in basking in reflected glory. They wanted what George wanted. And George quickly realized that he wanted a second chance. He returned to Old Trafford a few weeks later, and although he was alone this time, he was better prepared to cope with the experience. (McMordie didn't get another chance at United, though he did go on to play professionally.)

When Matt Busby finally got to see the subject of Bishop's telegram on the pitch, he made an extraordinary decision. The United boss instructed the coaching staff not to try and teach Best anything. To put that into perspective, Bobby Charlton had arrived at Old Trafford as a marvellously gifted young player, yet by no means the finished article. Coaches had to instil in Charlton the importance of the short game, when he wanted to spray long raking balls all over the park. Busby astutely recognized that Best's precocious talent had to be carefully nurtured, then given its head at the right moment.

George had to join United as an amateur, for the Irish FA was very concerned by the top English clubs poaching the country's most talented youngsters. It meant that George had to

have a regular job, and he was installed as a lowly clerk with the Manchester Ship Canal Company. George was mortified. He had come to Old Trafford to play football, not to be a tea-boy. In the event United neatly sidestepped the regulations by putting him to work in an electrical supplies store. The shop owner was an avid United fan and willingly allowed Best - along with John Fitzpatrick - to head off to the training pitch after putting in just a token appearance at work.

Youth team star

The next two years were spent playing in United's junior ranks. By the start of the 1963-64 season Busby once again had an exciting youth side on his hands, with Best as its star. The team went on to beat Swindon Town 5-2 on aggregate in the FA Youth Cup Final that season, the club's first victory in that competition since 1957. Jimmy Rimmer, David Sadler, John Aston and John Fitzpatrick also played in that team. But while they were gradually promoted through the ranks, Busby recognized that Best's scintillating performances made him one for the present, not the future.

In the 1963-64 season Best was not only the star of the side which won the Youth Cup, but he broke into the United first team and won his first full cap for Northern Ireland.

European Footballer of the Year

Busby had signed George as a full professional on his 17th birthday, in May 1963, and handed him his Division One debut just four months later, on 14 September. He performed creditably in the game, in which the opponents were West Bromwich Albion. Playing on the right wing, George found himself up against an experienced full back in Graham Williams, who was a Welsh international. Honours were fairly even on the day, Best feeling that he hadn't really done himself justice.

He had to wait more than three months for his next taste of first-team action. The call came after United suffered a 6-1 defeat by Burnley at Turf Moor on Boxing Day. George, who had gone home for Christmas, was summoned to return to Manchester. He was in the side for the home game on 28 December. The opponents were Burnley again, giving United a swift opportunity to avenge their recent mauling. Best gave a dazzling display in a 5-1 victory. He gave Burnley full back Alex Elder a torrid time throughout, and cappped his performance with his first goal for the club. He was a permanent fixture in the team thereafter.

First international honours

Just four months later, on 15 April 1964, Best was awarded his first international cap. Having been overlooked by Northern Ireland at schoolboy level, 21 appearances for United had convinced the selectors that Best was ready to step up to international level. He helped Northern Ireland to a 3-2 victory over Wales at Swansea. He was just 17 years 328 days old. Making his debut in the same match was the man who would go on to become a goalkeeping legend, Pat Jennings. Unlike Jennings, however, Best would become increasingly disillusioned and frustrated with international football. He was unfortunate in that his career spanned a lean period in Northern Ireland's fortunes. He was 12 years old at the time of Northern Ireland's glorious World Cup campaign of 1958; he was 36 by the time the country next won through to the finals, Spain 1982. Best's major achievements, therefore, were destined to be at club level.

He had his first taste of FA Cup and European competition in his debut season. United were holders of the FA Cup and looked a good bet to go all the way again when they eased their way into the semi-final. But Busby's men went down 3-1 to West Ham, and Best missed out on the chance of becoming the youngest player to appear in a Cup Final. Ironically, that honour went to Howard Kendall in the same year. Kendall, who was born on the same day as Best - 22 May, 1946 - was in the

Preston side which won through from the other semi-final before losing to West Ham at Wembley. Still short of his 18th birthday, Best might not have regarded this is an irretrievable calamity. However, he was to suffer a string of FA Cup disappointments - several at the semi-final stage - and failure to appear in the Wembley showpiece was to be one of his great regrets.

The disappointment in the 1963-64 FA Cup paled beside the team's exit from the Cup Winners' Cup. Drawn against Sporting Lisbon in the quarter-final, United took what seemed to be a stranglehold on the tie by winning the home leg 4-1. The return leg came just four days after the West Ham game, and a lacklustre United found themselves on the receiving end of a 5-0 mauling. The club's misery was complete when Liverpool pipped them for the championship. Within a matter of days a glorious treble had evaporated.

Rapier-like wing play

On a personal note, the 1963-64 season had seen Best rise from the relative obscurity of the juniors to become a regular first-teamer with a growing reputation. That reputation reached stratospheric proportions after one particular performance early the next season. It was a league match at Stamford Bridge against a Chelsea side which Tommy Docherty had moulded into one of the most exciting young outfits in the country. United won the game 2-0, with Best pulling all the strings. Ken Shellito, who had been capped by England at full back, was the defender on the sharp end of Best's rapier-like wing play. After he had spent 90 minutes cutting the Chelsea defence to ribbons, the whole stadium - fans and players alike - applauded him off the field. The 18-year-old admitted to feeling awkward and abashed at having the spotlight turned on him. He was supremely confident in his ability, and had that arrogant streak that is so often the hallmark of performers at the top of their game; yet by nature Best was actually rather shy.

Best inspires United to title victory

The remainder of Best's first full season for United continued in much the same vein. And while he raided down the left wing, John Connelly performed brilliantly on the right. Connelly had arrived from Burnley at the back end of the previous season in a £50,000 deal. With two wingers in devastating form, strikers of the calibre of Law and Herd, and Charlton in a new withdrawn role, United moved up a gear. The nearly-men of 1963-64 won the championship from Leeds on goal average. Best's

performances - not to mention a highly creditable 10 goals - had helped to bring the Division One title back to Old Trafford for the first time since 1956-57. The season had had its disappointments - the team fell at the semi-final hurdle in both the FA Cup and the Inter-Cities Fairs Cup. However, the championship meant another crack at the European Cup, the trophy Busby was so desperate to win.

The trappings of success

Off the field Best was beginning to enjoy the trappings of success. From earning just over £4 when he arrived at Old Trafford, rising to £17 when he turned professional, Best was now on a basic wage of £125 per week. With bonuses and the commercial offers that began rolling in his actual weekly income was in four figures. Not an insubstantial sum even by today's standards, in the mid-1960s it represented a small fortune.

As far as extra-curricular activities were concerned, by 1965 there were already early signs of Best pushing the boundaries and challenging authority. It was fairly tepid and predictable stuff in the early days. Ten-pin bowling was a particular favourite, though that had more to do with the young girls that congregated there than any particular love of the game. Drink wasn't a major issue either; often nothing more than Coke was consumed. Later, almost inevitably, came the desire to burn the candle at both ends. It was natural enough for many young men in their late teens. For Best - a good-looking, high-profile sportsman with money to burn - the lure of the party circuit was irresistible. He swapped his Austin 1100 for a succession of sports cars, E-Type Jaguars being a particular favourite. That did nothing to hinder the 'pulling power' in which Best and his circle took such a keen interest.

Enjoying the club scene

Best never really developed a taste for alcohol. Certainly early experimentation with beer and lager was very short-lived. On the other hand, he enjoyed the pub and club scene, and he liked the effect of the booze. He was still the shy Belfast boy at heart and he wanted an alcoholic drink that he could enjoy on his nights out. The answer was vodka and lemonade, where the alcohol was masked but none the less potent for that. It was to become his favourite tipple.

There had already been recriminations for the lifestyle Best had adopted. At one point the club had cause to impose a curfew on him at Mrs Fullaway's, where Best lodged for many years. He found himself on the carpet in front of Busby on a number of occasions. In the early part of the 1965-66 season the United boss even dropped him from the team. However, as a young, ultra-fit athlete Best was able to accommodate the carousing and it had little effect on his performance on the pitch. He could also train hard - there were no disappearing acts at this stage.

Busby the father-figure

Busby had a self-confessed soft spot for George. He could be ruthless with players who underperformed, challenged his authority or whose actions reflected badly on the club. Johnny Giles's swift exit from Old Trafford after speaking his mind was a prime example of Busby's rod-of-iron approach. With Best,

however, he would admit to being a somewhat indulgent father-figure. Even when the worst excesses came later, Busby's soft spot for George never really hardened; he was always ready to believe that his wayward star had finally mended his ways.

If Best was riding high in 1964-65, his profile went onto a different level altogether the following season. The launch pad which catapulted him beyond the back pages, which saw him as likely to feature in news, pop and fashion items as anything to do with football, was the European Cup. More specifically, it was the quarter-final tie against Benfica.

The Portuguese team had taken over Real Madrid's mantle as Europe's premier side. They had reached the European Cup Final four times in the previous five years, winning it twice. In the process they had won 18 consecutive European ties on home soil, scored a hatful of goals and conceded very few. The fact that the Stadium of Light was a virtual fortress suggested that United were on their way out of the competition, for they went to Lisbon with only a narrow 3-2 victory from the Old Trafford leg to defend.

'El Beatle'

For once Busby urged caution in his team talk. Best had other ideas. He scored a brilliant header after six minutes, then added a second after a dazzling run in the 12th minute. When he laid on a third for Connelly on the quarter-hour, the tie was effectively over. The final scoreline of 5-1 had Busby purring, with Best singled out for special praise. The pre-match instructions may have gone in one ear and straight out the other, but Busby couldn't be harsh with a player who had single-handedly destroyed the opposition in the first quarter of the game.

Best awoke next morning to find that the headline writers in the Portuguese press had dubbed him 'El Beatle'. They acknowledged that Best had totally eclipsed their own star and newly crowned European Footballer of the Year, Eusebio. He returned home sporting a large sombrero to milk the theme. The British media turned out in force to get the picture and the story. George Best was no longer simply a sporting star, he was a celebrity.

European disappointment

The consensus of informed opinion holds that United's 1965-66 team should have realized Busby's European Cup dream. Most agree that the side was at its peak around this time. The season ended in great disappointment, however. In the semi-final United were matched against Partizan Belgrade, a physical but quite ordinary side. Busby was desperate for his match-winner in Lisbon to carry on in the same vein in Belgrade. Unfortunately, Best had picked up a knee ligament injury which required an operation. It was a huge decision, for this was an era where no substitutes were allowed. Best was desperate to play, Busby desperate to play him, and they gambled. It backfired. Best's knee went early in the game, leaving him a passenger as Partizan won the game 2-0.

It was the end of Best's season. He was a frustrated spectator for the return leg, where United could manage only a 1-0 win. To make matters worse, the team faltered in the League and finished 4th. Having looked a good bet to win the European Cup,

United would now have to wait until 1968 at the earliest to have another crack at the coveted trophy.

The 1965-66 season had ended prematurely through injury, but Best had done enough to be awarded 3rd place in the Footballer of the Year poll. That was no mean achievement, considering he was up against England's World Cup heroes. Bobby Charlton took the top honour, with George Cohen second. There was more compensation for the recent disappointments in the staggering success of Best's off-field ventures. By now he had an agent, Ken Stanley, who was inundated with lucrative commercial offers. Best also made his first foray into the business world by opening a boutique, Edwardia, in Sale.

Back to full fitness

By the start of the new season Best was back, fully fit and firing on all cylinders. He was an ever-present in a side which won the championship for the second time in three years. With no European distractions, and a 4th round exit from the FA Cup, United were able to focus all their efforts on winning the League. Law was again top scorer, on 23. Best weighed in with 10 goals, another excellent strike-rate for a winger.

Busby had paid Chelsea £55,000 for Alex Stepney at the beginning of the 1966-67 season to solve the thorny goalkeeping problem. He became one of just three big-money signings in the side that won the championship, the others being Crerand and Herd. The rest of the side had come through United's ranks, with several of the 1963-64 Youth side finally making the breakthrough into the first team to join Best.

Goalscoring responsibility

Law and Herd had provided the focal point to United's attacks for several seasons. In 1967-68 Best emerged as the top striker - out of necessity as much as anything. Herd broke his leg in March 1967, and although he made a full recovery, the 33-year-old found himself sidelined, being replaced by another of United's burgeoning talents, Brian Kidd. Law's season was severely curtailed through injury and suspension. A concerned Busby made enquiries about several proven goalscorers, including Geoff Hurst and Jimmy Johnstone. They came to nothing. It was Best who took the goalscoring responsibility on his shoulders. He hit 28 in the League, making him the club's top marksman for the first time. He was also the Division One hotshot, along with Southampton's Ron Davies. Best's goals weren't quite enough to help United retain their title, though. Manchester City pipped them for the championship on the last day of the season.

And so to the European Cup campaign of 1967-68. Shunning false modesty, Best is clear about the magnitude of his personal contribution. Quite simply, he believes United wouldn't have triumphed without him.

Best's decisive goal

A 4-0 aggregate victory over Hibernian of Malta gave United a comfortable passage into the second round, where they faced Sarajevo. This was a bruising encounter. United came away from Yugoslavia with a goalless draw in a game most notable for marking the club's first plane journey since Munich. They got through by virtue of a 2-1 win at Old Trafford. Aston scored the first after the Sarajevo 'keeper failed to hold a Best header, then Best himself grabbed what proved to be the decisive goal.

The Irishman was on the scoresheet again in the quarter-final, against Polish side Gornik. United were well on top but struggling in front of goal in the home leg. It was Best who made the breakthrough after leaving a couple of defenders in his wake. Kidd scrambled home a second in the dying minutes. Busby was worried that the team was too heavily dependent on Best's flair and unpredictability. He decided that 2-0 justified a rearguard action in Poland. United were beaten 1-0; it was enough to put them into the semis once again.

Beating the Spanish giants

Their opponents were Real Madrid. The Spanish giants weren't the force they had been, but then - Best apart - neither were United. Best scored with a thunderous shot from an Aston cross in the home leg, the only goal of the game. Busby opted to drop an out-of-sorts Law and play an extra defender in Madrid. That tactic had to be abandoned at half-time as United came in 3-1 down. Sadler was pushed forward in the second half and he scored to reduce the deficit. With time running out, Best picked up the ball and went on a typical mazy run near the touchline. He looked up and saw - of all people - centre-half Bill Foulkes charging forward. Best picked him out perfectly and Foulkes slotted the ball home to put United into the final.

Champions of Europe

The opposition for the Wembley showdown on 29 May was Benfica once again. Eusebio was still there, but the Portuguese side was another which was in decline. After 90 minutes the score was 1-1, Graca equalizing Charlton's glancing header. It was no classic, but the fireworks were kept back for extra-time. Best ignited the touch-paper early in the first period. When Kidd flicked on a Stepney clearance, Best was onto it in a flash. He beat Cruz, then rounded 'keeper Henrique before passing the ball into the empty net. Kidd and Charlton completed the extra-time rout and made the final scoreline 4-1. Best had done more than anyone to deliver the European Cup that had been Busby's driving passion for more than a decade.

Best's avalanche of goals and dazzling displays in 1967-68 earned him the British and European Footballer of the Year awards. At 22 he was the youngest player ever to receive the latter honour.

Bursting onto the scene

Previous page: Wingers were regarded as goal providers when Best burst onto the scene. He created countless chances for others, but was a regular on the scoresheet himself right from the outset. He grabbed 10 goals in his first full season, 1964-65.

Right: Brilliant performances on the pitch and a pop star image off it make Best a magnet for young autograph hunters.

Below right: 24 August, 1964. Best skips round West Ham goalkeeper Jim Standen in United's 3-1 defeat at Upton Park. United would lose just six more games on their way to the championship

Below: Best sports the Beatle look in 1964. The 'El Beatle' tag which catapulted him into the superstar bracket came 18 months later.

Stamford Bridge applauds the new star

Above: Best pictured shortly after his devastating performance in United's 2-0 win at Chelsea on 30 September, 1964. At the end of what was a one-man demolition job on Tommy Docherty's highly-rated young side both sets of players and the whole of Stamford Bridge applauded him off the pitch.

Left: 1964-65 was Best's first full season in the United team. He was in sparkling form throughout, helping the club to their first championship since the Babes' era.

Opposite: Model professional. Best was increasingly in demand for fashion photo-shoots.

Making the headlines

5 March, 1966. Best in action in the FA Cup 5th Round tie against Wolves at Molyneux. He scores the pick of United's goals in a 4-2 victory. The team's Cup hopes were dashed by Everton in the semi-finals.

Opposite top: 12 March, 1966. Relaxing with Bill Foulkes (left) and Harry Gregg at a West End hotel as United prepare to take on Chelsea at Stamford Bridge. United went down 2-0 on this occasion.

Opposite below: Daily Mail sports columnist Ian Wooldridge focuses his attention on Best the footballing genius. It wasn't long before George began making headlines on the front pages as well.

Superb balance, perfect control

5 November, 1966. Best is on top form as United beat Chelsea 3-1 at Stamford Bridge. His superb balance and control leave Eddie McCreadie and Bobby Tambling tackling thin air. McCreadie recovers to make a second challenge, but can only stop the quicksilver Irishman by fouling him.

September 1966. Best's flair and creativity aren't confined to the football pitch. Here he puts the finishing touches to some of his own designs prior to a fashion show at Tiffany's nightclub in Manchester.

Trimming the famous locks

Left: Fame and fortune allow Best the luxury of a personal hairdresser. Linda Gidman trims the most famous locks in football at his Chorlton-cum-Hardy digs, with David Sadler looking on.

Opposite: At 20 Best had it all. The partying had already begun, but at this stage it took no toll on his ability to train hard and play brilliantly.

Above: Best lodged with Mary Fullaway at 9 Ayecliffe Avenue, Chorlton-cum-Hardy for more than ten years, off and on. When he and drinking partner Mike Summerbee wanted to 'entertain', they used a flat which they had acquired for the purpose.

Fashion advice

November 1966. Sidelined by injury, Best takes the opportunity to spend some time in his boutique in Sale. 19-year-old actress Sue Whitman gets some fashion advice from the most celebrated shop assistant in the land.

Opposite top: Holidaying in Majorca became a summer ritual for Best. In July 1967 he and Mike Summerbee bumped into boxer Johnny Prescott, who joined their hectic party schedule.

Opposite below: 25 November, 1967. With the inevitable attractive blonde in tow, Best arrives at Euston Station en route for the latest battle of Stamford Bridge. The game ends in a 1-1 draw.

And good in the air...

Right: Best's terrific spring made him just as big a threat in the air as on the deck.

Opposite: Arch-rivals on the pitch, Best and Manchester City's Mike Summerbee were close friends off it. The two fashion-conscious stars joined forces to open their own boutique, Edwardia, in October 1967.

28-goal hotshot

Below: January 1968. When League champions United are drawn against Cup holders Spurs in the 3rd Round of the competition, the papers can't resist making the most of Best's fashion connections. United failed to get the measure of Spurs, who left Old Trafford with a 2-2 draw, then won the replay at White Hart Lane.

Below right and opposite top left: February 1968. Best shows off his 'special' new girlfriend Jackie Glass, the latest in a long line of leggy blondes that he was involved with. 'I don't believe in engagements,' says 20-year-old Jackie. Just as well.

Right: Best puts his feet up during his golden season. Apart from his enormous contribution towards United's European Cup triumph, he was also the team's top scorer with 28 League goals. He was also the Division One hotshot that season, along with Southampton's Ron Davies.

Opposite bottom right: 24 April, 1968. United players embrace after their 1-0 win over Real Madrid in the first leg of the European Cup semi-final. Best scored the goal which gave United a slender but vital advantage to take to the Bernebeu Stadium.

Opposite bottom left: Best pivots and swivels, and another defender fails to make acquaintance with the ball. Such skills earn him the Football Writers Footballer of the Year award. He polled 60% of the votes cast, and at 21 became the youngest player ever to receive the honour.

Opposite top right: Model professional. By the mid-1960s Best was inundated with lucrative commercial offers. Here he is seen on a photo-shoot for Great Universal Stores. The contract was worth a staggering £20,000.

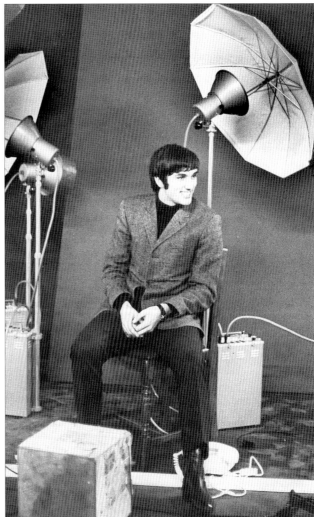

Footballer of the Year

16 May, 1968. Best becomes the third United player to win the Footballer of the Year award in its 20-year history. The others were Johnny Carey (1948-49) and Bobby Charlton (1965-66).

Opposite: The new Footballer of the Year enjoys an impromptu game of cricket with some of his neighbours' children.

King of Europe

Crerand, Best and Busby battle their way through the crowds at Euston Station, clutching the coveted trophy.

Opposite above left: 16 May, 1968. Best sports a matador-style hat on his return from United's 3-3 draw against Real Madrid, a result which put them into the European Cup Final.

Opposite above right: 'Best holds all the aces for the European Cup Final against Benfica.' The photo-opportunity prior to the big game had a certain irony to it, for Best was to become addicted to gambling as well as alcohol.

Opposite below: The world's most famous young footballer gets help in choosing the right kit.

Star in a declining side

The decline in United's fortunes after the Wembley triumph was dramatic, and had huge implications for Best. With the powers of Law and Charlton beginning to wane, the Irishman was undoubtedly the jewel in the club's crown. He needed quality around him. Busby had had to recall 36-year-old Foulkes for the European Cup Final, yet his only purchase in the summer of 1968 was another forward, Willie Morgan. Best was unimpressed by the £100,000 acquisition from Burnley. United had never finished worse than 4th in the League in the five seasons since Best had broken into the first team. Suddenly, he found himself the star of an ordinary side which had to settle for mid-table mediocrity. It was something he found difficult to come to terms with. For years he had been the idol of the terraces, endured the pressures that came with pin-up boy adulation and experienced the most intense media scrutiny. Now there was failure to contend with.

He was top scorer again, hitting 19 in the League, but United could only finish 11th. Beaten by Everton in the 6th Round of the FA Cup and AC Milan in the semi-final of the European Cup, the season was an anti-climax after the previous year's glories.

Indifferent performances on the pitch provided Best with an excuse to over-indulge off it. Up to the European Cup triumph, his drinking had been counterbalanced by the fact that he trained hard as part of a successful team. More often than not the drinking was celebratory. Now, playing in an average side, the booze became a refuge from mediocrity.

Best asked Busby to make him captain and rebuild the side round him. Busby refused, citing the Irishman's irresponsibility. Best assured his manager that he would rise to the challenge; Busby wanted evidence of a change of attitude and demeanour first. Concerned about Best's wayward lifestyle, Busby was keen for him to find a nice girl and settle down. Best responded by becoming engaged to a Scandinavian blonde, Eva Haraldsted, whom he had only recently met. Busby was horrified. Although the engagement was soon broken off, the whole affair merely affirmed the manager's view that his star hadn't mended his dissolute ways.

Early in 1969 Busby announced that he was handing the problem of Best and an ailing side to someone else. Wilf McGuinness was appointed from within to take up the poisoned chalice. He, like Best, recognized that new talent needed to be brought in. McGuinness had his eye on Colin Todd and Malcolm MacDonald, but was prevented from making a move for them. Instead, he had Arsenal's Ian Ure foisted on him. That was hardly likely to galvanize Best, yet he was once again the top scorer in 1969-70, hitting 25 goals in all competitions. United finished 8th.

With no top-class purchases and few quality youngsters coming through the ranks, United were still heavily dependent on Law, Charlton, Stiles - and, of course, Best. The side couldn't sustain a title challenge, but was capable of performing well in one-off situations. United got to the semis of both domestic cups in 1969-70. In these competitions Best provided classic examples of his sublime skills, and his petulance and irresponsibility. In the first leg of the League Cup semi-final against Manchester City at Maine Road, Best's temper got the better of him after United lost the match 2-1. He knocked the ball out of the referee's hands, for which he received a 4-week suspension and a £100 fine. In the 5th Round of the FA Cup, by contrast, he gave one of his most memorable performances, scoring six in United's 8-2 win at Northampton.

United went on to face Leeds in the semi-final of the FA Cup. The tie went to a replay at Villa Park. Before the game, McGuinness found Best in a compromising situation with a young girl. United survived with another draw, but were beaten when the teams met for a third time. It was ironic that Leeds - whose style and approach to the game was anathema to both Busby and Best - was now one of the most formidable sides in the country. United, by contrast, were languishing in mid-table.

Best's increasing unreliability mirrored the team's declining fortunes on the pitch. Having been refused the captaincy and accused of irresponsibility, he began living up - or down - to that tag. Matters weren't helped when he discovered that Law and Charlton were still being paid more than him. In the heady, successful days Best had never quibbled about the terms of his contract. Now, with Law and Charlton shadows of their former selves and the team on the slide, he felt aggrieved and undervalued.

The 1970-71 season was much the same: continued mediocrity on the pitch, a frustrated Best bingeing after training - or sometimes instead of it. Yet he still managed to finish top scorer for the fourth successive year.

The mounting problems briefly landed back at Busby's door, for he took over the reins again after McGuinness was sacked in December 1970. One of his first duties back in the hotseat was to accompany Best to an FA Disciplinary Committee hearing for the number of bookings he had accumulated. Best rolled up late, for which he was given a hefty fine and a ban. He then failed to turn up for an away match at Chelsea early in the new year. A furious Busby set off with the team, leaving word for Best not to bother travelling to London. Best was indeed in the capital that weekend - visiting actress Sinead Cusack.

Yet another carpeting and suspension followed, but Best was soon restored to the team. It was hardly surprising; having bought just one forward in six years - Willie Morgan - United couldn't afford to do without the 21 goals that he supplied.

Ten years after arriving in Manchester, Best finally got round to swapping his digs for a house of his own. Predictably, it was a bold, individual design, built at a cost of £35,000. The ultra-modern property afforded him no refuge from the public and media gaze. A stream of visitors came to gawp at their hero's abode. Best rarely stayed there, and the house was sold within two years.

A long way from Wembley

The British and European Footballer of the Year shows off his silky skills in the surf to Danish holidaymaker Karna Anderson in Magaluf, Majorca.

Opposite: Best had plenty to smile about in 1968. He was top of the footballing tree and commanded a 4-figure weekly income when the average wage was nearer £25. The 67-68 season was the high-point in Best's career. United went into rapid decline thereafter, and Best's increasingly erratic behaviour mirrored the team's waning fortunes.

A hat-trick for George

Opposite: July 1968. A 6-month driving ban means that Best has to resort to pedal power for the cameras at least.

Another hat-trick for George, this time while holidaying in Majorca in the summer of 1968.

If it's June it must be Majorca. Best was part of a set whose summer-long routine consisted of lying on the beach all day and partying all night.

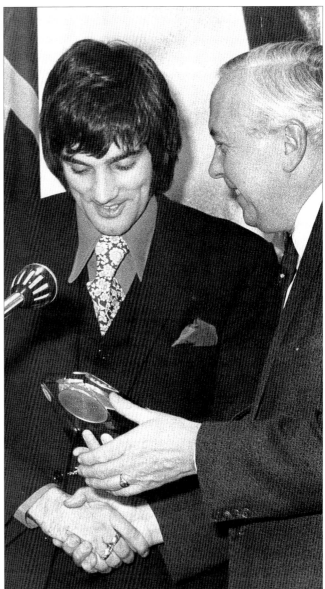

Life in the fast lane

Opposite below: Best employs a chauffeur to take the wheel of his Jaguar. Julia Somers is interested in the job, but the peaked cap goes to Bill White.

Left: Best in action during the 1968-69 season. He was top scorer yet again, but Busby's failure to strengthen the side saw United slump to 11th in Division One.

Opposite above: Best spent his money as fast as he made it. Cars were among his many costly indulgences. Here he takes the wheel of the ultimate in 60s motoring chic, the Mini Cooper S.

Above: 25 November, 1969. Prime Minister Harold Wilson presents Best with his award for finishing 3rd in a Sportsman of the Year poll. He finished behind Tony Jacklin and Lester Piggott.

Busby–'Settle down George'

Opposite: Best responds to Busby's exhortations for him to 'find a nice girl and settle down' by becoming engaged to Eva Haraldsted. He had spotted the 21-year-old Danish blonde among a crowd of autograph hunters during United's pre-season tour to Copenhagen. News of their engagement leaves Busby aghast.

Best's engagement to Eva Haraldsted is over almost before the champagne goes flat. 'I'm not the marrying kind,' says George. 'I might find it difficult to be faithful.'

After the engagement is broken off, Eva Haraldsted sues Best for breach of promise. He settles out of court for £500. The couple subsequently bump into each other at a nightclub and engage in some turntable taunting. She asks the DJ to play 'I'm Leaving On A Jet Plane'; George requests 'Get Back To Where You Once Belonged'. Things turn ugly when Paddy Crerand is accused of breaking the jaw of Christopher Todd, Eva's escort on the night in question.

Below: 20 September, 1969. Best is in devastating form during United's 2-2 draw at Highbury. He scores one, and makes the other for Sadler.

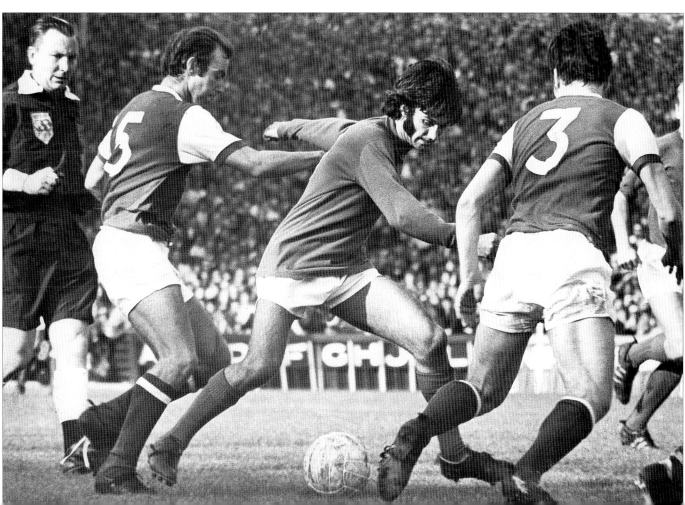

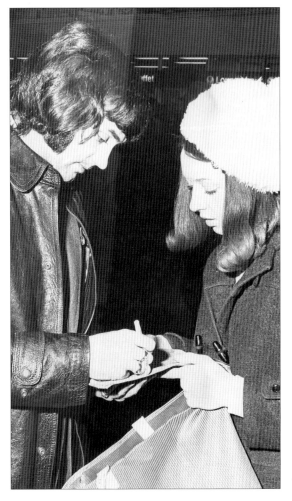

Best's premier fan

Best arrives at 10 Downing Street for a reception held by Prime Minister Harold Wilson. The Premier's constituency was in Liverpool, but that didn't stop him being a huge Best fan.

Opposite below left: George obliges yet another fan. His appeal encompassed old and young, male and female alike. The pressures on him were, accordingly, so much the greater.

Opposite above: January 1970. Best starts a 28-day ban imposed following an incident at the end of the League Cup semi-final defeat by Manchester City on 3 December. United announce they will be applying to the FA for permission to pay Best during the ban. Not that he will be on his uppers during his enforced lay-off. He is reported to have been offered £1000 per week to do ball juggling in a nightclub. 'I'm interested,' said Best, 'as long as it doesn't involve too many late nights.'

Opposite below right: In a snowbound Manchester Best is serenaded by singer Lucy Farrington, who had written and recorded a song dedicated to the United star. He had plenty of time on his hands to listen following his four week suspension.

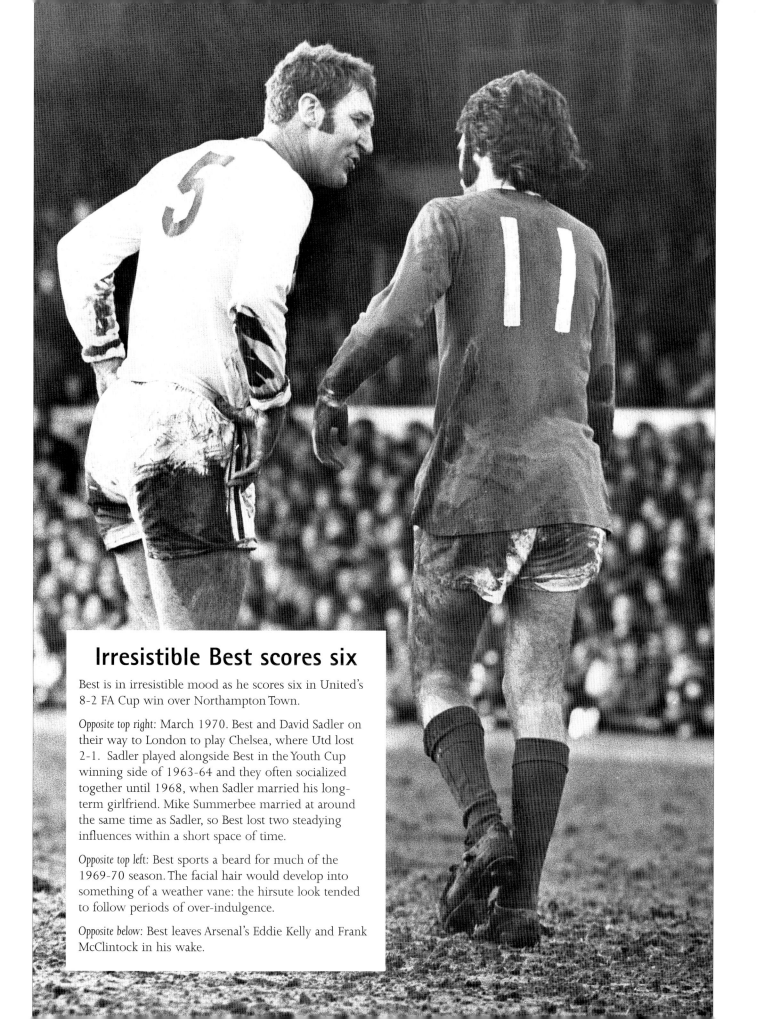

Irresistible Best scores six

Best is in irresistible mood as he scores six in United's 8-2 FA Cup win over Northampton Town.

Opposite top right: March 1970. Best and David Sadler on their way to London to play Chelsea, where Utd lost 2-1. Sadler played alongside Best in the Youth Cup winning side of 1963-64 and they often socialized together until 1968, when Sadler married his long-term girlfriend. Mike Summerbee married at around the same time as Sadler, so Best lost two steadying influences within a short space of time.

Opposite top left: Best sports a beard for much of the 1969-70 season. The facial hair would develop into something of a weather vane: the hirsute look tended to follow periods of over-indulgence.

Opposite below: Best leaves Arsenal's Eddie Kelly and Frank McClintock in his wake.

'He was unplayable'

The opposition may not have been the strongest, but Northampton were riding high in Division 4 and had fancied their chances of causing an upset. Their plans came unstuck as they found Best at his most mercurial. He had just served a month's ban, during which time United had been unbeaten. Some had even questioned the wisdom of restoring him to the side. Northampton manager Dave Bowen said after the game: 'I wish they'd given him five weeks. No side in Europe could have stopped him.' Fairfax, the Northampton defender charged with shadowing Best agreed. 'He was unplayable. I'd rather face Pele any day.'

Opposite: In action during the 1969-70 season, McGuiness's only full term at United's helm. Best was unhappy with the team, yet still produced many magical performances and was again top scorer, hitting 25 goals in all competitions.

United in decline

Opposite: April 1970. A policeman takes Best's name, but this time it's only as a fan. An earlier brush with authority hadn't been quite so amicable. Best had been sent off for throwing mud at the referee during Northern Ireland's defeat by Scotland.

Below: 26 April. Best flies out to Bermuda to join his United team-mates in a 4-week tour. He had contributed hugely to United finishing in 8th place in the League and reaching the semi-finals of both cups. However, his and the team's problems were mounting.

Left: High-scoring jinks as Northampton are hit for six of the Best.

Back to mum and dad in Belfast

Below: Best returns home as his parents Dick and Anne celebrate their silver wedding anniversary in June 1970. His trips back to Belfast became increasingly rare, something which would cause him considerable guilt in later years.

Opposite: Anne Best was herself an alcoholic by the time she and husband Dick celebrated their 25th wedding anniversary. Unlike her son, Anne was teetotal until she was 40. She died in 1978, aged 54.

Right: August 1970. The new season begins disastrously for United. Best increasingly finds solace in parties and booze. And yet another Scandinavian beauty, Siv Hederby.

A £35,000 luxury home fit for the Best

October 1970. Best moves into his new £35,000 house in Bramhall, Cheshire. The ultra-modern, hi-tech property brought him little joy. A constant stream of fans camped outside, desperate to catch a glimpse of their idol or grab a souvenir. He sold the house two years later, having spent very little time actually living there.

The house was built to his own brief round a sunken bath and a room big enough to contain a full-sized snooker table.

The white-tiled unit contains a 25" colour TV set and stereo record player which can be elevated by remote control from a console by the main door to the lounge which also activates the electronically operated curtains.

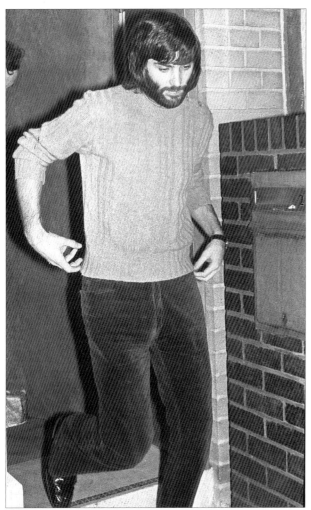

Record fine

Opposite above: January 1971. One of Busby's first jobs after taking over as manager again was to accompany Best to the FA hearing. The United boss anguished over his treatment of Best and whether he could have done more to keep him on the straight and narrow.

Best looks suitably contrite as he finally joins Busby for his FA disciplinary hearing at the Cavendish Hotel, London. He had missed his train southward, claiming he had been feeling unwell. Whether or not the Committee realized this was a euphemism for being hung over, they handed him a record £250 fine and a 6-week suspended sentence for the three bookings he had accumulated in the previous 12 months.

Left: Busby and Best set off for his appeal meeting the following month.

Opposite below right: Passing judgement. Best and Charlton were poles apart in terms of character and demeanour.

Opposite below left: 9 January, 1971. Best visits Sinead Cusack instead of turning up for United's game at Chelsea. The actress's Islington home is besieged by fans and the media for two days before Best returns to Old Trafford to face the music. Busby hands him a two-week suspension.

Above: Gorgeous blonde, beautiful car. There was a rapid turnover of models in both areas, but the formula remained the same. Best's companion of the moment is 21-year-old Terry Robinson, a member of the Young Generation dance group.

The Best-dressed man around

Left: Summer 1971. Best plays the role of the Englishman abroad when his company, George Best Boutiques, is floated on the Stock Exchange. He makes an instant paper profit of £3000.

Left and below: Clean-shaven and razor-sharp, Best rattles in 13 goals in 16 games between August and November, 1971.

The Old Trafford faithful saw Best in his pomp for the final time in the autumn of 1971. His performances and goals were instrumental in United's return to the top of the League for the first time in three years.

The arrival of Frank O'Farrell brought about a dramatic improvement in the autumn of 1971. Best was in great goalscoring form and United went back to the top of Division One. It proved to be a short-lived honeymoon, however.

Sent off

Right and below left: 18 August, 1971. United coach Malcolm Musgrove escorts Best from the pitch after he is sent off by referee Norman Burtenshaw at Stamford Bridge. His dismissal came after Peter Osgood laid on the first goal for Tommy Baldwin. Willie Morgan protested that Osgood had been guilty of pushing. Burtenshaw booked the United winger, then sent Best off after the latter remonstrated even more vehemently. United won the game 3-2.

Opposite and below right: September 1971. Best returns from an FA hearing following his sending off at Chelsea. Referee Norman Burtenshaw had dismissed him for using foul and abusive language. Best had claimed that Willie Morgan had been the target of his vitriol.

A relieved Best learns that the 6-week suspended sentence he had hanging over his head has been quashed. The Disciplinary Committee couldn't be sure that the abusive language was directed towards the referee.

Life after United

Frank O'Farrell's appointment as United manager brought a dramatic change of fortune in the early part of the 1971-72 season. The team was playing well, Best was in sensational scoring form and by December United once again topped the League. The transformation was illusory, and temporary. The early months of 1972 saw United go into free fall. In the middle of a string of defeats, Best was dropped after going AWOL yet again. He had opted for a tried and trusted combination of the bottle and another glamorous girlfriend, Miss Great Britain Carolyn Moore.

Top scorer again

O'Farrell made the usual attempts to crack the whip, but iron-ically, his best tactic was to strengthen the team. Martin Buchan's arrival from Aberdeen in March 1972 was a great fil-lip, and Ian Storey-Moore initially did well when he was bought from Forest. The rot was stopped, and United finished the season in 8th place, the same as the year before, with Best once again the top scorer.

It wasn't good enough for the Irishman. He announced his retirement at the end of the season. Although he retracted the decision a couple of weeks later, it was merely staving off the inevitable. O'Farrell committed the cardinal sin as far as Best was concerned: buying players he didn't think were good enough to wear the famous red shirt. United slid into the rele-gation zone and Best did another disappearing act. O'Farrell responded by putting him on the transfer list, but it was the manager himself whose time was up.

As United negotiated to bring in the charismatic Tommy Docherty, then manager of Scotland, Best's life was in turmoil. He was axed from a lucrative boot sponsorship deal, replaced by the young, talented - and clean-cut - Kevin Keegan.

Docherty reaffirmed O'Farrell's decision to sell Best, and he was transfer-listed again early in 1973. Best, trying to get his retaliation in first, announced once again that he was quitting the game. After an unsavoury nightclub incident, where he was accused of assaulting a waitress, Best had had enough. He flew out to America to investigate the possibility of playing out there. No deal was done at that point, and it turned into a leisurely holiday. He returned to Britain to sell off his bou-tiques, then, with no footballing or commercial commitments, prepared for a long leisurely summer in Spain.

A health scare cut all that short. Best developed a thrombo-sis in his leg and returned home for treatment. It was a window of opportunity which enabled fences to be mended. Prompted by Busby, Docherty re-signed him. Still only 27, Best found his appetite and enthusiasm for the game again. He trained hard as the 1973-74 season got under way, and by the end of the year he felt he was getting his sharpness back.

Last time at Old-Trafford

A New Year party proved to be his undoing. Best missed a training session, and quickly found that Docherty wasn't as indulgent as Busby had been. Although he made up for the session he had missed, Docherty dropped him for the follow-ing game. The new boss insisted that Best was left out because he turned up for the game the worse for wear, not because he missed training. Best vehemently maintained that he arrived for the match in good time, fit and cold sober. Best reacted belligerently. Neither of the volatile characters would cede any ground and Best left Old Trafford for the last time.

With time on his hands it was unfortunate that Best had just opened a nightclub, Slack Alice's, along with some business associates. It was there, early in 1974, that he met the reigning Miss World Marjorie Wallace. A brief liaison ended with Best's arrest on theft charges. These were subsequently dropped, and Best cashed in by selling the story of the affair to *The People*.

That philosophy certainly applied to a string of appear-ances for some of the lesser lights of the footballing world over the next few years. Between August 1974 and March 1983 he turned out for Dunstable, Stockport, Cork Celtic, Hibernian and Bournemouth. In each case Best was paid a hefty appearance fee, the quid pro quo being the fact that his name on a team sheet put bums on seats. It was tawdry, demeaning stuff.

Fulham with Moore and Marsh

His one serious effort with a British club in the post-United era was with Fulham. He linked up with Bobby Moore and Rodney Marsh when he signed for Bobby Campbell's Division Two side in August 1976. As ever, Best could turn it on in brief spells, but sustaining it over a long, gruelling British sea-son was something else. There were run-ins with referees on the pitch and a contractual dispute with Fulham off it. The solace of the bottle was never far away, and Best, now turned 30, could no longer brush aside the effects of the bingeing and turn in top-notch performances.

Fulham started well, then faded badly, finishing 17th in the league at the end of the 1976-77 season. Best lasted just 10 games of the new campaign before leaving Craven Cottage for good in November 1977.

The remainder of his playing career was spent in America. He had signed for Los Angeles Aztecs in December 1975, and for two years juggled his playing career between California and Fulham. After walking out of Craven Cottage, Best returned to the West Coast, playing well, albeit in an undemanding League. The drink was still flowing freely, and made even easier as he became part-owner of a bar that was renamed 'Bestie's.'

A United break

Opposite: November 1971. All smiles as Best, Aston and Sadler celebrate being back on top. The United players take a break in Jersey, three points clear at the top of the League. Note that Sadler enjoys a cigarette; Best's addictions never included tobacco.

Below: A hopeful young fan asks for Best's autograph.

United picked up where they left off on returning from their Jersey break. The team remained unbeaten throughout December 1971 and still topped Division One.

Opposite: April 1972. Carolyn Moore (left) is among the models at a Manchester fashion show organized by Best. Her tenure as Miss Great Britain would last a lot longer than her time as Best's latest beauty queen girlfriend.

Birthday boy

22 May, 1972. Celebrating his 26th birthday with friends in Marbella while all Europe was asking: 'Have you quit?'

Best's retirement from the game lasts just two weeks. By early June he had had a change of heart and patched things up with manager Frank O'Farrell.

Opposite above: June 1972. Best is back in Spain but this time he is soaking up the sun and relaxing in Majorca.

One of the few pictures of 'George and female companion' which wouldn't send the gossip columnists into overdrive. Having heard so much about Best's holidays over the past seven years, 60-year-old Mary Fullaway decides to see for herself what Majorca has to offer.

Off to the States

The increase in Majorca's popularity meant that it was no longer a sanctuary from Best's goldfish-bowl lifestyle.

Opposite top left: September 1972. Things may have been going badly on the pitch, but Best is still in big demand in the commercial world. Here he models the 'Bramhall quilted ciré nylon rally jacket'. With a retail price of £11, the manufacturers would have had to sell quite a few to cover Best's fee.

February 1973. While his ex-team-mates battle to avoid relegation, Best flies out to America. Negotiations to play out there come to nothing, and it turns into an extended holiday.

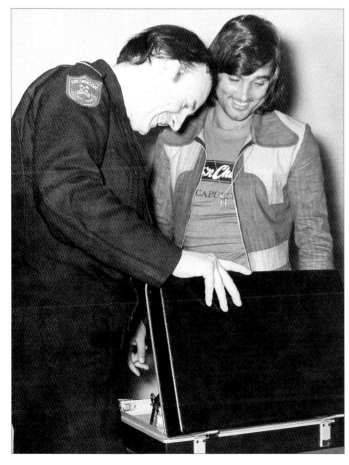

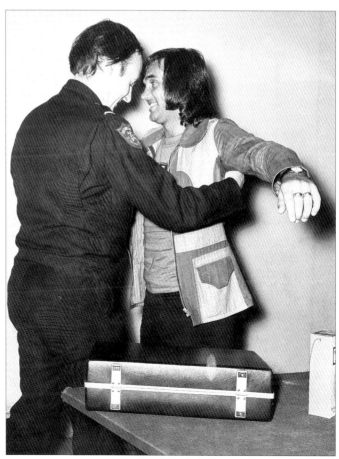

Hail the returning hero

Left: February 1973. Relaxing in a pool at a friends house in California.Best returns to Britain after a month's sojourn in America. Having turned his back on football, he now also sells his boutiques. Drinking is his main occupation for many months.

Below: 6 September, 1973. Best announces his intention to resume his playing career with United. Busby, ever willing to believe that Best had turned the corner, prompted Docherty to re-sign him. Best is seen here preparing to fly out to Lisbon for Eusebio's testimonial match with manager Tommy Docherty. Best was desperate for match practice as he battled his way back to full fitness. He would later accuse Docherty of playing him too soon. But it was all smiles for now. Docherty's big clear-out at United was something that Best thought was long overdue. Docherty hoped that Best's return after a 9-month lay-off would galvanize the new-look side.

Opposite top: 20 October, 1973. Hail the returning hero. Still struggling to regain his fitness, Best lasts half the game as United beat Birmingham City 1-0 at Old Trafford. He didn't cap his return to the team by scoring the goal, that honour went to Alex Stepney. United's goalkeeper was the team's penalty taker and was currently the club's joint top scorer on two.

Opposite below left: February 1974. Best leaves Tramp nightclub with reigning Miss World Marjorie Wallace. A few days later he is arrested and charged with theft.

Opposite below right: 24 April, 1974. The case against Best is dropped after Marjorie Wallace fails to turn up in court.

Playing for Southern League Dunstable

Opposite top left: August 1974. Ex-West Bromwich Albion and England striker Jeff Astle welcomes his new team-mate to Dunstable. Best dismisses the couple of games he plays for the Southern League team as nothing more than a favour to manager Barry Fry, an old pal from his early days at Old Trafford.

Opposite top right: A tanned, overweight Best turns out for Dunstable alongside a paint-sprayer, accountant and barrage balloon maker. The Southern League club's average gate of 400 rockets to nearly 4000. It is the first in a series of demeaning, 'circus show' spectacles.

Opposite below: It's a communal bath and brown ale after Best helps Dunstable to a 3-2 win. His £500 fee made it an expensive win for Barry Fry's side.

Above: March 1975. Best is still some way short of his 30th birthday, but Michael Parkinson has more than enough material for his biography. The two are pictured promoting the book on Pete Murray's Radio 2 show *Open House*.

Right: August 1976. A new club and wedding bells in the air. Best checks the back and front page coverage watched by Angela Janes.

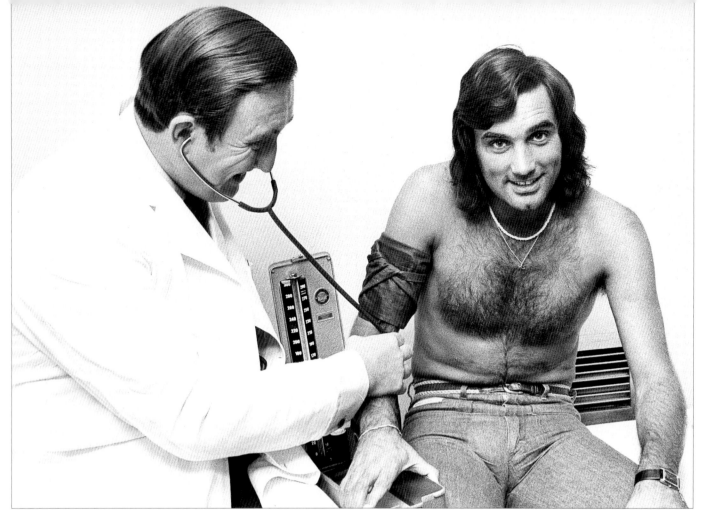

King of Craven Cottage

Above: 21 August, 1976. Fulham manager Bobby Campbell introduces his new signing to the Craven Cottage fans before the team's opening Division Two match against Nottingham Forest. With Best is his 23-year-old girlfriend Angela Janes.

Opposite below: September 1976. Best's new Fulham team-mates include Rodney Marsh, a £25,000 buy from Tampa Bay Rowdies.

Opposite above: A fit and lean Best has no trouble sailing through the Fulham medical. When the team's promising start fizzled out halfway through the season, he was back on the booze with a vengeance.

Left: Angela Janes may have been a model and Bunny Girl, but she was no doormat as the first Mrs Best. She once stabbed George during their tempestuous relationship. The couple met in May '76 in California. Angela, from Essex, has lived there for three years.

The big match

July 1976. George and Angela beside the Pacific at Hermosa Beach. 'The timing is just right. I am very much in love' said a delighted Best.

Opposite: Best scores on his debut for Fulham. Once again, fans turn out in droves hoping for a glimpse of his singular brand of magic.

Enduring Legacy

Best's girlfriend, Angela Janes, was from Southend. She had lived and worked in America for some time, first as a model, later as a personal trainer to the pop and film star Cher. They married in 1978 and had a son, Calum, in 1981. It was a stormy relationship, characterized by countless break-ups and reconciliations. Angie had to deal with Best's unfaithfulness, but it was his drinking which precipitated the final split, in 1982. They divorced four years later.

After leaving the Aztecs, there were stints with Fort Lauderdale Strikers and San Jose Earthquakes. The latter was the worst team in the North American Soccer League. Best had resorted to the bottle when United began to struggle; 10 years on, in his mid-30s, the booze was never far away now that he had plumbed the depths of the American game.

Searching for a challenge

There were periods of remission. After Calum's birth he admitted himself into a clinic to dry out. There was also an optimistic period in 1982 when, at 36, he entertained hopes of making Northern Ireland's World Cup squad. He had cleaned up his act many times when a challenge worthy of his attention presented itself. But his boredom threshhold was low, and he always lapsed into his old ways sooner or later.

Best's World Cup hopes were dashed. Instead of taking the field in Spain in 1982, he was faced with the break from Angie and Calum, and was experimenting with pills and implants to try and control his alcohol problem. Just when it seemed things couldn't get worse, the Inland Revenue hit him with a demand for unpaid tax of nearly £20,000. On top of everything else he now had the threat of bankruptcy hanging over his head. It would take him ten years, until May 1992, to discharge the debt and lift that burden from his shoulders.

Jailed for drink-driving

Although Best had made a fortune, a combination of poor investments, bad advice and a champagne lifestyle had left him living a largely hand-to-mouth existence. There was the occasional large casino win and some lucrative pay-days for appearance work, but Best had few assets. Money always had a habit of slipping through his fingers with consummate ease.

The nadir for Best came in December 1984, when he was jailed for three months. He had been stopped for drink-driving,

then failed to turn up in court. A warrant was issued for his arrest, and Best sealed his own fate by assaulting a policeman. He was sent to Pentonville first, then on to Ford open prison in Sussex for the rest of the sentence. Best was shaken by the degradation and ignominy of prison life, and made sure he earned maximum remission. On his release, in February 1985, he headed off to Mauritius with his latest love, Angie Lynn. The trip was paid for by *The Sun*, to whom George had sold the story of his time inside.

Back from the brink

Like Angie Best before her, Angie Lynn had a rollercoaster relationship with Best. After their final break-up, in the autumn of 1986, George embarked on an 8-year relationship with the woman he said brought him back from the brink. Mary Shatila became not just his partner but also manager of his business affairs. She recognized that he was still a very bankable name, and was the driving force behind his move into the lucrative after-dinner circuit.

George and Mary came close to marrying several times, but by 1994 the relationship had run its course. In the summer of that year he met the woman who was to become the second Mrs Best, Alex Pursey. She was a 22-year-old flight attendant with Virgin Airlines when they met, at Tramp nightclub. They married a year later.

The pain and the heartache

Best was approaching 50 when he married for the second time, yet he had mellowed little. The same irresponsibility which had prevented him from gaining the United captaincy was still in evidence. He was always liable to turn up for a professional engagement the worse for wear - or not at all. The short fuse was still there, too - he and Alex admitted to engaging in the odd bout of fisticuffs. And his weakness for a pretty face, a roll of the dice and an alcoholic beverage was undiminished.

But the charm and magnetism have accompanied him into middle age, too. And - most importantly of all - the affection in which he is still held by football fans everywhere. More than affection; reverence. Sir Matt Busby said that he could forgive Best the pain and heartache he caused because of all those magical, uplifting moments of breathtaking virtuosity on the pitch.

And when all else is stripped away, that is the enduring legacy. He played the beautiful game. Beautifully.

Aztec George

Opposite far left: Best pictured at London Airport in January 1977. His commitments to Fulham and the Aztecs necessitated a lot of long-haul commuting during this period.

Opposite left: September 1977. Best heads to Belfast to play for Northern Ireland against Iceland. The dispute between the LA Aztecs and Fulham may have been settled in the latter's favour, but Best soon votes with his feet, the lure of the West Coast proving too great.

Above: February 1980. Angie Best quickly discovered that wedding vows had little impact on George's predilection for alcohol and infidelity.

Previous page: Surrounded by a bevy of beauties at his testimonial dinner. Marriage to Angie the following year failed to curb his roving eye.

Calum Best

1981 saw Best drinking heavily and reduced to playing for San Jose Earthquakes, one of the worst teams in the North American Soccer League. One of the few bright moments was the birth of his son Calum.

Opposite: Calum's arrival failed to have a sobering effect on Best. Angie's tolerance was exhausted by 1982, although the couple didn't divorce till four years later.

Below left: George cools off during the Superstars Past Masters competition, held at Oxford.

Below right: George tries his hand at canoeing during the Superstars competition. He didn't take to it well and withdrew from the event.

George with his new love and having a ball

Right: July 1982. Best and his new love, ex-Miss World Mary Stavin, attend the Berkeley Street Ball.

Opposite above: The final ignominy of Best's playing career came in March 1983, when he turned out for Third Division side Bournemouth.

Opposite below: February 1984. George joins forces with a host of female celebrities to launch a series of Shape Up And Dance LPs. Pictured with George are (left to right): Patti Boulaye, Suzanne Dando, Mary Stavin, Lulu and Bucks Fizz singer Jay Aston.

Below: Angela Best flies into London giving George a chance to see 18-month-old Calum. 'I don't want to talk about George. I'm over here on a business and pleasure trip. It's great to be home again. I'm having talks about doing a TV series and I am getting back to modelling.'

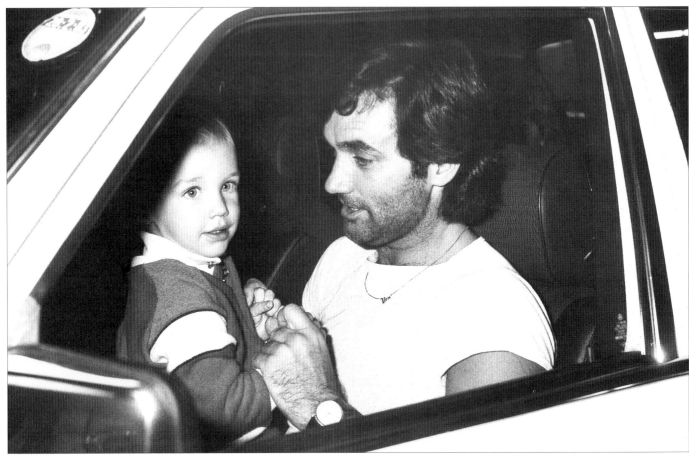

With son Calum, March 1984. Although Calum is brought
up mainly in America with Angie, football is his abiding
passion. His ambition is to play professionally, preferably for
Manchester United.

It was soon after this time that Best went to Scandinavia to
have pellets of the drug Antabuse implanted in his stomach.
Drinking now had potentially fatal consequences.

George goes to prison

Left: Even with a prison sentence hanging over his head for drink-driving and assaulting a policeman, Best remains a big draw on the commercial front. Here he signs footballs at the opening of a London sports shop.

Below: December 1984. Having had his appeal dismissed, Best is driven off to Pentonville, where he spends the first few days of his prison term.

Below left: January 1985. Best shuffles round the compound of Ford open prison with the rest of the inmates. He finds it a totally degrading experience and ensures that he earns maximum remission.

Below right: January 1986. A year on from his own incarceration at Ford open prison, Best organizes a celebrity team to take on an inmates XI at Bognor.

'I was top scorer for six seasons'

George and Angie's turbulent marriage officially ended in July 1986. She believed Best was in a spiral of decline and did not want to be dragged down with him.

Opposite: June 1987. Some nightclub eventually had to throw together one of Best's past partners with the present incumbent. A year on from their divorce, Angie Best looks happy for George and his new love, Jan Locke.

Above left: You never lose it. A decade on from their Fulham days Best and Marsh team up for a TV series in which they pick out some of their golden footballing moments. Both agree that the modern game is lacking in the kind of individuality and flair that was their hallmark.

Above right: Like so many before her, Mary Shatila couldn't curb George's drinking, gambling and womanizing during their eight years together. She did manage his business interests very shrewdly, however, and was responsible for putting his financial affairs in order.

Right: August 1990. 'I get tired of hearing that I blew it too early. I was top scorer for United for six seasons.'

'I achieved everything'

August 1990. Best reflects on the merits of Paul Gascoigne while sitting at a bar, naturally. He dismisses the hype surrounding Gascoigne and is less than impressed by his performances, including those at Italia '90. 'Twenty years ago he would have been another average midfield player. By the time I was 22 I'd achieved everything. Gazza, at 23, has proved nothing yet'.

Opposite: George and Mary Shatila enjoy a night out at the London Palladium. Russ Abbot provided the laughs, though Best still had bankruptcy hanging over his head.

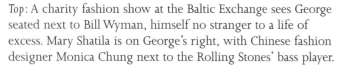

Top: A charity fashion show at the Baltic Exchange sees George seated next to Bill Wyman, himself no stranger to a life of excess. Mary Shatila is on George's right, with Chinese fashion designer Monica Chung next to the Rolling Stones' bass player.

Right: June 1993. George and Mary Shatila attend a memorial service for Bobby Moore at Westminster Abbey.

Opposite above left: January 1993. Best regards Mary Shatila as the woman who brought him back from the brink.

Above: Back at the Theatre of Dreams as a commentator in 1992-93.

Players are afraid to be different

On the road with Rodney Marsh. Best invariably needs lubrication to get him through the gruelling schedule of the road shows. Marsh occasionally has to prompt his partner, and has been known to tell some of George's anecdotes himself. 'Football in the late 80s is a grey game played by grey people,' says Marsh. 'Today people take it all so seriously,' adds Best. 'You never see anyone laugh during a game. Maybe it's the pressure. It makes players afraid to try anything different.' Best assures audiences that his shows with Marsh are unscripted with a gag at his own expense. 'Of course they are. For one thing we never know from one night to the next if I'm going to turn up.'

Reflecting on the record: 178 goals in 466 games for Manchester United

December 1993. Best feels that under Alex Ferguson's guidance Ryan Giggs will avoid the kind of pitfalls which saw him out of top-flight football by the age of 27. The comparisons were inevitable. Among all the subjective viewpoints regarding the relative merits of Best and Giggs, two facts, at least, stand out. One is Best's prolific goalscoring record - he notched 178 goals in his 466 games for United. The other is the fact that Best was the British and European Footballer of the Year at the age of 22.

The beard may be greying and the waistline thickening but the 48-year-old's eye for a beautiful girl is as keen as ever. His new love is 22-year-old air stewardess Alex Pursey.

Opposite: 25 July, 1995. George and Alex end their wedding day celebrations at *Tramp*, where they met the previous summer. The new Mrs Best swaps her job with Virgin Atlantic for the demanding role of organizing George's business affairs.

Left: November 1995. Alex Best insisted that her husband shave off his beard. It made him look younger, she said, and exposed 'that sexy chin with a cleft like a baby's bottom'.